I0816937

CITIZEN SCIENCE PROJECTS

Butterfly Projects

BY KARI A. CORNELL

Kids Core

An Imprint of Abdo Publishing
abdobooks.com

abdobooks.com

Printed in the United States of America, North Mankato, Minnesota.
102025
012026

Cover Photo: Leena Robinson/Shutterstock Images
Interior Photos: Anne Katherine Jones/Shutterstock Images, 4–5; Bob Hilscher/Shutterstock Images, 7; William Cushman/Shutterstock Images, 8; Leo Kohout/Shutterstock Images, 10; Boonchai Wedmakawand/Moment/Getty Images, 12–13; Jay Ondreicka/Shutterstock Images, 15; Shutterstock Images, 17, 22, 25, 28 (bottom), 29 (top), 29 (bottom); LWA/Stone/Getty Images, 18; Molly Shannon/Shutterstock Images, 20–21; Yuliya Evstratenko/Shutterstock Images, 26; Leena Robinson/Shutterstock Images, 28 (top)

Editor: Trudy Becker
Series Designer: Marley Richmond

Library of Congress Control Number: 2025939132

Publisher's Cataloging-in-Publication Data

Names: Cornell, Kari A., author.
Title: Butterfly projects / by Kari A. Cornell
Description: Minneapolis, Minnesota: Abdo Publishing, 2026 | Series: Citizen science projects | Includes online resources and index.
Identifiers: ISBN 9781098298555 (lib. bdg.) | ISBN 9798384932352 (ebook)
Subjects: LCSH: Science projects--Juvenile literature. | Field experiments--Juvenile literature. | Butterflies--Juvenile literature. | Zoology--Experiments--Juvenile literature. | Lepidopterology--Juvenile literature. | Ecology--Experiments--Juvenile literature. | Ecological science--Juvenile literature.
Classification: DDC 507.8--dc23

CONTENTS

Butterflies are most active in the morning and midafternoon.

CHAPTER 1

Tagging Monarchs

Will and his sister Lily walked through the field. They each carried a butterfly net. As Lily took a step, she pushed aside purple wildflowers that towered over her head. Then she spotted a flutter of orange-and-black wings. It was a monarch butterfly!

Lily raised her net to try to catch it. But the butterfly zigged and zagged through the air. As the sun warmed the meadow, more monarchs appeared. Lily was sure she'd have another chance to catch a monarch.

Will and Lily were in Kansas. They were volunteering with Monarch Watch. This group helps track the travels of monarch butterflies. It was fall, so the monarchs were beginning to **migrate** south. Each year, the butterflies fly from Canada and the northern United States down to Mexico. After the long flight, they rest in pine trees. In the spring, the monarchs fly north again to lay their eggs.

The founder of Monarch Watch had taught the volunteers how to catch and tag monarchs.

Some monarchs travel as far as 3,000 miles (4,830 km) each year. They make stops along the way.

Monarch Watch tags are small, light stickers.

They can attach a small, round tag with a unique code to a butterfly's wing. Then, each time that butterfly is caught, volunteers can look at the code. They can record the butterfly's location on the Monarch Watch website. They can see where else that butterfly has been.

Will and Lily were excited to help. They knew Monarch Watch did important work. Monarch **populations** have been going down. But knowing where butterflies travel and stay is useful. Scientists can study these areas. This helps them learn how to protect monarchs.

A Long Journey

By April 2025, Monarch Watch had helped tag more than 2 million butterflies. Eduardo Rendón-Salinas is a scientist. He has reported finding Monarch Watch tags on the ground at monarch resting sites in Mexico. The monarchs had traveled from much farther north.

Sometimes so many butterflies cling to a tree that the branches sag under their weight.

Citizen Science

Monarch Watch's tagging program is an example of citizen science. Citizen science is when regular people help gather **data** about the natural world. In many projects, people observe things in nature and report what they see. The information they gather helps scientists in their research.

Further Evidence

Look at the website below. Does it give any new evidence to support Chapter One?

Monarch Butterfly

abdocorelibrary.com/butterfly-projects

Helpers who are monitoring butterflies can bring notebooks to record their findings.

CHAPTER 2

Counting Butterflies

Many citizen science projects focus on butterflies. For example, people can report when they first see butterflies in the spring. They can count butterfly eggs and **larvae**. This data helps scientists find ways to protect butterflies and their **habitats**.

It also provides key information about butterfly populations.

Monarch Larva Monitoring

The Monarch Larva **Monitoring** Project (MLMP) is one butterfly project. Volunteers across North America count monarch butterfly eggs and larvae. They also keep track of milkweed. Milkweed is key to monarchs' habitats. It is a host plant. Butterflies lay their eggs on

All about Milkweed

Milkweed plants come in many varieties. In the fall, pointed pods release fluffy white seeds. When a milkweed leaf or stem breaks, milky white liquid oozes out. This is how the plant gets its name.

Monarch eggs are usually a creamy yellow color.

milkweed plants. When the eggs hatch, growing caterpillars eat the plants' leaves.

MLMP volunteers find an area to monitor. First, they count the number of milkweed plants in the area. Then they check each plant for eggs.

They search for larvae too. They look all over the plant, including under the leaves. Then they record the number of eggs and larvae.

Citizen scientists count the number of monarch butterflies in the area too. Volunteers return to the site on the same day each week of the growing season. Then they submit all their notes on the MLMP website.

Butterfly Counts

In butterfly count programs, volunteers count all **species** of butterflies they see. The Xerces Society held a major count in 1975. It was known as the Fourth of July Butterfly Count. Later, the North American Butterfly Association (NABA) took it over.

Life Cycle of a Butterfly

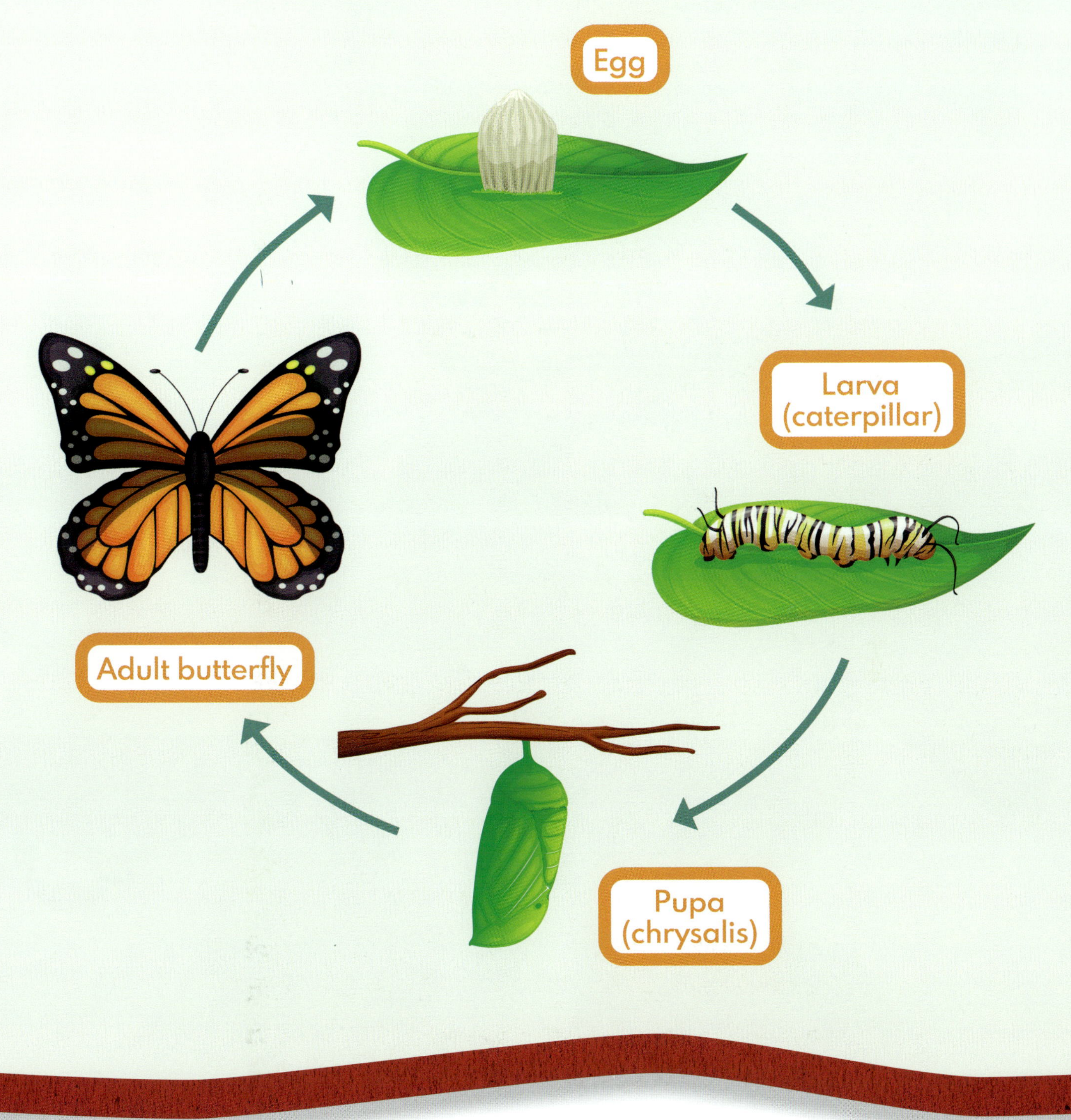

A butterfly goes through many different stages during its life.

Binoculars can be useful tools for spotting butterflies far away.

The organization holds several butterfly counts each year. Hundreds of groups participate. These groups are called circles. Each circle counts all the butterflies they see in a certain area.

Explore Online

Visit the website below. Does it give information about milkweed and monarchs that wasn't in Chapter Two?

Milkweed for Monarchs

abdocorelibrary.com/butterfly-projects

People can help butterflies find food by growing flowering plants in addition to grass.

CHAPTER 3

Helping Butterflies

Butterfly populations need a steady food source to stay healthy. The plants that butterflies use for food and **nectar** vary by butterfly species. People can help butterflies by planting gardens with some of these plants.

Some people create small gardens on their windowsills. Passing insects can stop at the flowers.

These gardens should include a variety of flowers that butterflies use. People can plant them in their backyards. Or they can pot them on patios or small balconies. Even small gardens can provide a habitat for butterflies.

Host Plants

Volunteers planning a butterfly garden should include at least three host plants. Milkweed is the only host that monarchs use. The blooms also provide nectar for migrating butterflies.

However, planters have many options besides milkweed. Several swallowtail butterfly species eat parsley. Painted lady caterpillars eat mallow and thistle. False nettle is food for red admiral caterpillars. Clouded sulphur butterflies eat blue false indigo. All of these plants are great to include in a butterfly garden.

Nectar Plants

Some plants in butterfly gardens should provide nectar to butterflies. Some great options are native thistle, goldenrod, and butterfly weed. Others to consider are joe-pye weed, New England aster, zinnia, or gaillardia. Planters can get ideas from local garden stores that sell native plants. Many volunteers try to

Butterfly Garden Certification Program

Gardeners can apply to have NABA approve their butterfly gardens. Gardeners must plant at least three different caterpillar host plants. Gardens must also have at least three different types of nectar plants. And people cannot use harmful chemicals. These products can kill butterflies.

Buttonbush plants provide food for eastern tiger swallowtail butterflies.

plant flowers that bloom at different times. That supplies nectar throughout the season.

Citizen scientists can take many actions to help butterflies. They can grow useful habitats. They can gather data about butterfly travels.

Citizen scientists doing butterfly projects should handle the butterflies with care.

They can count eggs and larvae. Scientists use all this data to study butterflies. The work of citizen scientists will help protect butterflies in the future.

Primary Source

Karen Klinger works at the Field Museum in Chicago. She said:

> We found that monarchs can find the milkweed, wherever the milkweed is, even if it's in planters on balconies and rooftops. . . . Any milkweed garden can contribute habitat for monarchs.

Source: "Monarch Butterflies Need Help, and a Little Bit of Milkweed Goes a Long Way." *Field Museum*, 31 July 2024, fieldmuseum.org. Accessed 2 June 2025.

What's the Big Idea?

Read this quote carefully. What is its main idea? Explain how the main idea is supported by details.

Science Projects

Citizen scientists tagging for Monarch Watch need to order tagging kits online.

Citizen scientists recording data about monarch larvae need to submit their findings on the project website.

Citizen scientists signing up for butterfly counts in their areas need access to the North American Butterfly Association website.

Citizen scientists planting a butterfly garden need the right plants and spots to place them.

Glossary

data
information

habitat
the natural environment where a plant or animal lives

larva
a young insect that looks very different from its adult form

migrate
to move regularly from one place to another

monitor
to watch or keep track of

nectar
a sweet liquid produced by plants

populations
the numbers of individuals in certain areas

species
a group of similar living things that can produce young with one another

Online Resources

To learn more about butterflies and butterfly projects, visit our free resource websites below.

Visit **abdocorelibrary.com** or scan this QR code for free Common Core resources for teachers and students, including vetted activities, multimedia, and booklinks, for deeper subject comprehension.

Visit **abdobooklinks.com** or scan this QR code for free additional online weblinks for further learning. These links are routinely monitored and updated to provide the most current information available.

Learn More

Bell, Samantha S. *Animal Migration*. Abdo, 2026.

Bell, Samantha S. *Pollinator Gardens*. Abdo, 2026.

Davidson, Lauren. *Butterflies for Kids*. Rockridge, 2021.

Index

About the Author

Kari A. Cornell is an award-winning children's book author who gardens, runs, and makes pottery. She lives in Minneapolis with her husband and their sweet dog, EmmyLou.